Mishia Bee

Behind the Smile

Compiled By: Mishia Bee

Contributing Authors
(in order of appearance):

Fatima Wood
Jasmine Talisha
Chavon Winston
JessMarie
Jasmine Hubbard

Pearly Gates Publishing LLC
INSPIRING CHRISTIAN AUTHORS TO BE AUTHORS
Pearly Gates Publishing, LLC, Houston, Texas

Behind the Smile

Copyright © 2018
Mishia Bee

All Rights Reserved.
No portion of this publication may be reproduced, stored in any electronic system, or transmitted in any form or by any means (electronic, mechanical, photocopy, recording, or otherwise) without written permission from the publisher. Brief quotations may be used in literary reviews.

ISBN 13: 978-1-947445-38-3
Library of Congress Control Number: 2018961452

For information and bulk ordering, contact:
Pearly Gates Publishing, LLC
Angela Edwards, CEO
P.O. Box 62287
Houston, TX 77205
BestSeller@PearlyGatesPublishing.com

With Sincerest Gratitude

In no particular order, I would like to thank the following:

FATIMA

CHAVON

JASMINE T.

JESSICA

JASMINE H.

Each of you were brave enough to let your guard down and share your truth with the world through the telling of your story. You are the true definition of **BRAVERY** and **COURAGE**!

Thank you for joining me on this journey. I can't think of any other women I'd want to walk this walk with me.

I love each of you and thank you for the sisterhood we have created!

~ Mishia Bee ~

Introduction

Everything in life has a season. There's a season for animals to mate. There's a season for fruits and vegetables to be both sown and harvested. There's a season for trees to blossom and another for the leaves to fall. There's also a season in life when it's time to be **FREE** from the pains of the past.

Behind the Smile has been published for this season of renewal and release in your life. The authors who have penned their stories herein—*Mishia, Fatima, Chavon, Jasmine T, Jessica, and Jasmine H.*—have come to the realization that there is a need to not only tell their stories, but also share them in a way that lets you know: **YOU ARE NOT ALONE.** Through tears and thoughts of turning away from this project, they are the women who remained—and they are all the more stronger today than their yesterday.

As you ride this rollercoaster of emotions, know that the accounts shared here are real. You may find yourself cringing, crying, and even shaking your head in disgust as you come to relate to the former plights of the authors.

OH, BUT WAIT!

By the end of each horrifying account, you are sure to be empowered and enlightened as you come to embrace each as your own tale of being an overcomer!

Smile! With **ALL** glory given to God: Your **BEST** is yet to come!

Behind the Smile

Table of Contents

With Sincerest Gratitude vi

Introduction vii

~ Mishia Bee ~ 1

    Never Get Tired from Chasing Your Dream 2

    Mishia Bee ~ Dedication 13

~ Fatima Wood ~ 14

    Peace Begins with Telling My Truth 15

    Fatima Wood ~ Dedication 25

~ Jasmine Talisha ~ 26

    A Yunik Journey 27

    Jasmine Talisha ~ Dedication 38

~ Chavon Winston ~ 39

    Double Jeopardy 40

    Chevon Winston ~ Dedication 52

~ JessMarie ~ 53

Not All Scars Are Visible 54

JessMarie ~ Dedication 63

~ Jasmine Hubbard ~ 64

Seeking My New Normal 65

Jasmine Hubbard ~ Dedication 76

~ Mishia Bee ~

Mishia Bee is a 27-year-old entrepreneur. She is the Founder and CEO of a cosmetic line called "Bee U Cosmetics". (www.beeucosmetics.com)

Mishia Bee was born and raised in Southeast Washington, D.C. She loves giving back and also loves being a mentor to young women. Her goal is to show the younger generation that it's never too late to realize their dreams.

Mishia Bee

Never Get Tired from Chasing Your Dream

"**G**raduate high school." "Go to college." "A degree is what you need to get a good **JOB**," they said. That's all I ever heard as I entered high school. No one ever told me to save money, start a business, or anything like that. I had to figure out those things on my own.

Who would have ever guessed I would be 27 years old with my own thriving business? How did I get here? How did I manage to finish high school while taking ten classes during my senior year, just so I could graduate on time? I ask myself those questions often.

Following is my story behind acquiring the titles of CEO and Founder.

To begin, I was never the 'school type.' I didn't know how to study properly. I struggled with taking tests. School just wasn't for me. My last year of high school, I unexpectedly had to relocate to Waldorf with my godparents and godbrothers in order to graduate on schedule. (I was put out of my charter school because I didn't attend the mandatory summer school. My only options were to move in with them OR repeat the 11th grade—and that was something I was **NOT** going to do.)

When I first moved to Waldorf, I cried **EVERY** night. I missed home and wanted to move back. I was a city girl, and my new home was far too quiet for me. My godmother has always been my shoulder to cry on, my ear to listen, and the one who told me when I was wrong. My very first night at her house, she had a pep talk with me about how my upcoming school year was going to go. To this day, I can easily recall her exact words: "You're going to either love me or hate me, but your ass is going to graduate!"

That I did—and **ON TIME**, even though I had to take seven classes while in school, two classes after school, *and* a summer class. Ten classes? How, Mishia?! It was a struggle! My godmother helped me through it all by giving me her 100%.

So, what happened after graduation? I got pregnant! I didn't care, though, because I thought I was in love and that we were going to be one, big, happy family. Yeah…about that: **I WAS WRONG!** I sat down and reevaluated my "situation." I knew I wasn't ready for a baby—let alone with him—so, I got an abortion. I moved on from the guy I got pregnant by and decided to take a different path in life. I chose to return to school to obtain a degree.

I attended Everest College and received an Associate's Degree in Criminal Justice. **I DID ABSOLUTELY NOTHING WITH THAT DEGREE!** If I knew then what I know now, I would have invested in myself. I excuse my decision by noting that I was only 19 years old at the time. I didn't know what I wanted to do with my life, so I worked and went to school. I knew I had to work to get what I wanted. I managed to always maintain a job, but that wasn't fulfilling enough for me—even at the age of 19.

I partied **EVERY** day of the week (like an *average* 19-year-old). I used to come in the house at 2, 3, or 4 in the morning and jumped right up for school or work that same morning (like an *average* 19-year-old). Baby, I was **LIT**! I did that until I was about 23 years old.

When I was 23, I moved out on my own and got into a new relationship. Once again, I thought I had myself a real-life love story. All the clubbing and partying came to a screeching halt for a while because he and I were stuck together like Velcro. You saw him; you saw me. He was everything and more in my life. He was so handsome and sweet (at first). He was attentive, loved me, wanted to see me happy, and was just all around perfect...***for me***. I was in love! The beginning of our relationship was a little rocky, but once I got my own place and he got his, we didn't leave each other's sight unless duty called and we had to work. I was always at his house or he was always at mine. I was living a real-life fairytale! We were even trying to have a baby! Crazy, right?

Well, I didn't get pregnant for whatever the reason (thank God). After a few months, things between he and I changed drastically. We argued and fought. Our relationship started falling apart. I found out he was cheating on me. He would stay at his son's mother's house until 6 or 7 in the morning. It was crazy! I couldn't deal with the disrespect any longer, so I left him. Of course, the separation wasn't easy. We even tried to work it out again about a year later, but it just wasn't the same. We were over for good. I had to refocus and get my mind back on my goals because when I was with him, he had **all** of my attention.

As women, we get like that sometimes when we think we're in love.

Nonetheless, my focus returned—but not like it should have. I started going back out, having parties and sleepovers at my house, and basically did **WHATEVER** I wanted to do **ONCE AGAIN**. I used to go to the club thinking, "Oh, I'm 'bout to get me a **NEW** man!" I wasn't completely over my ex, so I thought getting a **NEW** man would help me get over the **OLD** one. (That lasted for a split second because dating these days is harder than I thought.)

In all honesty, I haven't been in a relationship since that breakup, and that was five years ago.

Still, I longed for that loving feeling again—minus the cheating, fussing, and fighting. I liked being a girlfriend. I liked coming home to someone every night. I liked talking about my day at work. In a nutshell, I loved to love.

After a few months, I considered returning to my mother's house because I hated being alone. I disliked the lonely feeling, but going back to mother's home would mean I wouldn't be free like I had gotten used to. I chose to stay in my own space. **That's** when I became a *woman*.

I stayed in my **OWN** place where I paid my **OWN** rent and my **OWN** bills. Now, don't get me wrong: I struggled, but I struggled with a smile on my face. My mother demonstrated the true definition of independence, so I never depended on anyone to do **ANYTHING** for me.

Okay. Let's fast-forward to July 2016.

I had my apartment for three years until tragedy struck. I returned home from work one day and saw my apartment building had caught on fire! I didn't know it happened until I pulled up and saw all the fire trucks, ambulances, and Red Cross volunteers surrounding my particular building. (It must be noted here that I wanted to move out because management was **THE WORST** to deal with, but I didn't want to **HAVE** to move out that way.) I was at a loss for words. I was given $300.00 and instructed to call my renter's insurance company to file a claim. Guess what? **I DIDN'T HAVE RENTER'S INSURANCE!** I couldn't afford to carry the coverage, so I let it lapse. I lost E.V.E.R.Y.T.H.I.N.G! I didn't know what to do.

I took a leap of faith, though. I called my prior insurance company, State Farm, and told them what happened. Basically, their response was, "You're out of luck!" I cried and prayed every day until they called me back and issued me a Case Manager. She reviewed my policy information and told me she would see what she could do for me. I was grateful for her efforts and decided not to wait to get a moving truck to remove my belongings from the apartment. I had to make a move!

Let me tell you how **God** worked things out in my favor. When I picked up my phone to call and see how much a moving truck would be, my Case Manager was calling. She said to me, "Okay. Send me a list of everything you lost. We are going to take care of it." Lord! I could've cried if I didn't already! LOL! She processed my claim and got me moved out in a timely manner. A check was cut so that I could recover those items I lost in the fire. I couldn't thank God enough. I bought a few things with the money, but Baby: I needed a *vacation*!

The claim was processed around my birthday, so I booked a trip to Jamaica and went **BY MYSELF**! That was one of the best vacations I have ever taken. I really enjoyed myself, but I knew reality was waiting for my return home.

Once I was back stateside, I moved back in with my mother. I was depressed, only because I told myself long ago I never wanted to go back home. I loved being on my own, but God had other plans for me.

Fast-forwarding another year…

In July 2017, I quit my job with no alternative plan in place. I hated my job and needed to get away from the toxic environment ASAP. It was probably a bad move, but

I didn't care, although I am one who always think about the "what ifs". Still, that didn't stop me from moving forward with my decision to quit. I was unemployed for about three months. In September, I began working a seasonal position—one I stayed at until April 2018.

PAUSE! Let's go back to *February* 2018.

That month, I had my very first mental breakdown. My mother and I had a bad falling out, so I moved. My job was ending soon and I had no savings. I was very depressed. I went to my godmother's house, sat on her couch, and cried for hours. All she did was hold me and tell me everything was going to be okay. I asked her, "How can you say that at a time like this?" She responded, "*Just WATCH!*" To be honest, I did **NOT** want to hear her typical words of encouragement **AT ALL** in that moment! I stayed at her house for a few days until I could get my head back on straight...well, at least a little straighter.

When I left my godmother's house after those few days, I went to stay at a friend's house. I stayed with my friend for a few months, but I hated feeling like I was in her way, so I went *back* to my mother's house.

Fortunately, everything between my mother and I returned to normal by then. Still, I wasn't feeling like myself. I concluded that I wanted to leave everything and everyone behind. I had no children, no man, and nothing holding me back from walking away from it all.

In March 2018, I realized I wanted to move to **LAS VEGAS**. I had my mind made up. I wanted to be on the other side of the country, away from everything and everyone. I told my godmother my plan. **SHE WAS NOT WITH IT AT ALL!** Still, she wanted to see me happy, so she leaned to accept my choice. My intent was to use my tax return money and start a new life in Las Vegas. I was so serious about the move that I made trips there for job interviews and went house-hunting. **I WAS NOT PLAYING!**

One day, my godmother said, "Mishia, you should start your own makeup line." I was like, "WHAT? How am I going to do that?" Well, she walked me through everything step by step. (I didn't realize at the time that her plan was to keep me from relocating. LOL!) Guess what? It worked! I saved all my money from my taxes and invested in myself.

July 2018 was when my life changed **FOREVER**! I became CEO and Founder of my very own cosmetic line called "Bee U Cosmetics." It is doing *very* well. I can't thank God and my godmother enough. After every lesson...after every "bad decision" I've made, it all paid off for me.

The message for everyone reading this is: **IT'S NEVER TOO LATE!** Stay focused and determined. Reach for the stars. Make your dream your reality.

If anyone would've sat me down and told me I would have my own company at the age of 27, I would have laughed and told them, "NOT ME!" I didn't believe I could do it. That's the biggest failure right there; believing you can't do it! **YOU CAN!** Whatever you put your mind to, **YOU CAN DO IT!** Nothing is ever too big to conquer. Any dreams you have, **CHASE THEM!** Yes, the journey will get hard, but don't give up! **KEEP PUSHING!** There's always a rainbow after the storm!

As for me, my future is looking bright! Be on the lookout for "Bee U Cosmetics"—coming soon to a town near you! If you can't wait, visit my website:

www.beeucosmetics.com

Mishia Bee ~ Dedication

I first want to thank God for giving me the strength to overcome my obstacles. I also want to thank and dedicate my chapter to my godmother. She has been my rock since day one. I love you, Benita! You mean the world to me!

Lastly, I want to dedicate this chapter to anyone who thinks their dream is too **BIG**. Nothing is ever too big! **CHASE THAT DREAM!!!** ♥

~ Fatima Wood ~

Fatima Wood is a 27-year-old mother of two. She was born and raised in Washington, D.C. in the Southeast area. She enjoys writing short stories and poetry.

Fatima is currently writing an urban novel. She is a survivor and wants to use her story to encourage women—young and old— to speak up and speak out for themselves, no matter what!

Peace Begins with Telling My Truth

As a pre-teen, I thought hanging around the older girls was the lit thing to do. I'd always ask my big sister if I could go "this place" or "that place" with her and her friends. We would do things like ride the 92-bus line around different neighborhoods, hang out at her friend's house, play fight on the playground, or just chill out on the corner somewhere. Whatever we did was cool with me. As long as I was feeling 'grown', I was with it.

I would often watch the way my sister and her friends acted, talked, walked, and dressed so that when I went home, I would pretend to be just like them while viewing my reflection in the bathroom mirror. I remember one time when I had on my sister's lipstick, a pair of her big earrings, one of her half-shirts, and a pair of her Parasuco jeans, I thought I was hot stuff as I walked back and forth in front of the mirror. About two minutes into my self-made fashion show, my aunt stormed through the door, yelling and screaming at me for what seemed like *forever* about me having my sister's clothes on and trying to be grown. Believe it or not, that didn't bother me because I felt that if my big sister could do it, look cute, and be popular, why couldn't I? I looked up to my sister and wanted to be just like her when I turned her age.

I could tell, however, that my aunts didn't really want me to hang around my sister and her friends. I guess that was because they were older and to them, I was already too grown for my age.

This one particular day, I heard my sister on the phone with her friend. I listened while they planned their whole day out. They had planned to catch the bus on the top of the hill to go to Shoe City and then grab a bite to eat at McDonald's. As soon as my sister hung up the phone, I was already in her face begging her to let me hang out with them. She eventually agreed to let me tag along—and even let me wear a pair of her jeans and a few of her bracelets!

After hanging out in the neighborhood all day, it started to get dark. On a normal day, my curfew would have been to be in the house before the street lights came on, but because I was with my big sister, I could return home whenever she did. As darkness fell, I guess my sister had asked our aunt if we could spend the night at one of her friend's houses (my sister always got her way, so of course the answer was 'yes').

This was the first time I ever spent the night at this

particular friend's house. I was thrilled because my sister would spend virtually every weekend there and then come home with stories to tell her other friends that were so exciting! One thing I did know about this friend's house was that it was the "turn-up house." This night was no different, and I was there!

When we arrived, my sister's friend's parents were leaving, so that meant we would have the house to ourselves and could do whatever we wanted. We headed downstairs to the basement along with a few other people who were already there. The space was dark, except for the blue light coming from a lamp on a table that dimly lit the room. Someone turned on the music and we all started dancing to The Back-Yard Band. Before I knew it, the dancing turned into a full-blown party! My sister's friend's brother invited his friends over, which actually made me feel a little uncomfortable because my big brother was among that crowd. Some of the girls were dancing on the boys while their friends sat back and cheered them on. The 'Freak Party' (as we called it back then) went on for a long time before people started to leave. **Finally**, it was just us girls again.

I recall staying up very late and listening to the

conversations my sister and her friends were having. While I did have my own group of friends, we didn't talk like the older girls at all. This group of girls I was with on this night talked about boys and things they had done with them. Some of the things they said were unthinkable to me at the time. I knew I wasn't ready to do any of **those** things. I mean, I had a little boyfriend back then, but all we did was talk and give each other a little peck on the lips when nobody was watching. Most often, he and I would shyly smile when we saw each other.

As the older girls' conversations continued, they talked about girls they didn't like and even about girls they hung out with who weren't there at the time. Some of the girls they talked about were among those who had just left the party. I remember being really quiet because, of course, I didn't have anything to say. I didn't fit in because I was just a little girl to them. I didn't care, though: I was **STILL** there!

After some time had passed, I got very sleepy. I suppose we all did because my sister, her friend, and I went upstairs and climbed into the bed. The girls who weren't staying over left, leaving just the three of us to sleep the remainder of the night away.

In the early hours of the morning, I woke up to find my sister and her friend were gone. They must have snuck out while I was asleep and just left me there. While still coming out of my sleep, I felt a light tap on my shoulder. I looked up and into the face of my sister's friend's cousin. I had seen him before but didn't really know him. We never really spoke, outside of the casual 'hello' in passing when he saw us outside. He asked me to go into the back room with him and, of course, my answer was "NO! Leave me alone!" I followed that up with an eye-roll. I had no idea what he wanted with me. He was much older than me and had no business saying anything whatsoever to me. He didn't take 'no' for an answer. He grabbed me firmly by the arm and said he just wanted to show me something. In that moment, I was so scared, I went with him.

I can clearly recall the room being very cold. There were no covers on the bed, yet he continually grabbed me by my waist to force me onto the bed. I kept pulling back, trying to walk away from him. I was nervous and started to feel a lump form in my throat that signaled I was about to cry. He got a hold of pants and because they were already a little too big, he was able to pull them down with just a few tugs.

He then laid me down on the bed. I remember crying, telling him to stop, and to leave me alone. He told me he wasn't going to hurt me and just to lay there and be quiet. I tried to move, but he was much stronger than I. I laid there and prayed that what I thought was about to happen wouldn't actually happen to me...again. "Not again... Not again..." played over and over in my head. I heard him as he used one hand to undo his pants while using the other to rub his penis on my butt for what seemed like forever. All the while, he was making all kinds of weird sounds, trying to be as quiet as possible.

I remember feeling so dirty and scared. So many things were going through my head. I felt like screaming but was too scared. I also thought about telling my sister's friend's mom as soon as my assailant went to sleep, but I was scared to do that, too. So, I just laid there and cried...in silence. After he finished his business with me, he used a small towel to clean me off. He then pulled my pants back up and walked me back to the room where I was peacefully sleeping before my childhood was ruined **once again** by a nasty, older guy.

Moments later, my sister and her friend came back into the room, trying to be as quiet as possible. After all, they weren't supposed to be out that late. They had no idea that if they had returned just a few minutes earlier, maybe that horrible thing wouldn't have happened to me.

My sister asked why I was awake and if everything was okay. I told her 'yes.' I don't know how I fought back those burning tears that day. I don't know if it was because I was scared or too shook up to tell her what had just happened to me. I do recall feeling like she might not believe me and that she would call me a **'LIAR!'** She might then accuse me of wanting to ruin her fun. So, I didn't say anything at all about the incident.

For the remainder of our stay at her friend's house, I couldn't help but wonder, "Why do these bad things keep happening to me? Why am I always the one chosen by these men? **I WAS A 12-YEAR-OLD CHILD!**" I didn't fall back to sleep that night. That was the first time I pulled an "all-nighter" (as the older people called it). I never expected my first all-nighter to be like it was. I laid in the bed with my eyes closed, wanting the morning to hurry up and come so I could go back home.

That was the **LAST** time I wanted to hang around older girls, spend the night at my sister's friend's house, or do any of the things they were doing that I felt were 'lit.' I just wanted to hang around my own friends and do the childish stuff we were doing, while hoping to **never** be violated again.

Looking back now, I still have a level of hatred towards older men. I have never dated an older man; neither have I ever spoken about any of the horrible things that happened to me as a child…before now.

For a long time, I blamed my sister. I didn't understand why she left me somewhere alone like she did. I wondered if she knew what was going to happen to me that night. I am also curious to know if her sister's friend did the same thing to her before because I felt like she asked me what was wrong because she **KNEW** something happened to me. I excused her, though, because she was just a teenager and didn't really look deeply into it.

Today, I feel that sharing my story will help another young woman realize she's not alone and that I have been in her shoes before. Furthermore, I want **all** women— young or old—to **never** keep quiet about sexual assault, whether it's from a family member, a friend's family member, or whomever. **It's not okay at all**.

I am now 27 years old with two beautiful children of my own whom I am very protective over because of situations like my own. Admittedly, now that I've written a part of my story and got it out, I am moreso at peace and can now begin to work on the *forgiveness* stage. I want to be able to forgive and move past my pain so that I can move forward with my life. This stage will probably be the hardest for me; however, I am ready and willing to because I am a strong woman. My troubled childhood no longer defines who I am today!

FE

Fatima Wood ~ Dedication

I dedicate this chapter to the ladies—young and old. Always speak out and speak up for yourself. Never let anyone take advantage of you in any kind of way. Your body is a temple, and no one deserves to disrespect it—**PERIOD!**

~ Jasmine Talisha ~

Jasmine Talisha is a Washington, D.C. native currently residing in Austin, Texas. After the death of her first daughter at a very young age, she's since been trying to maneuver her way through life as a mom and blogger.

Jasmine's story is a unique and tough one. Through her blog, she's learning to deal with her depression and anxiety, all while raising three beautiful children. She hopes to create a platform to reach others who may be in similar situations. She aspires to motivate, inspire, and uplift others. You can continue to follow her journey at: www.jasminetalisha.com.

A Yunik Journey

At the age of 20, I purchased my first piece of property. While that's a major accomplishment for most, it's definitely not what I had in mind at that age.

October 2008. That's when I met 'him.' He kinda "wowed" me, so we'll call him "Wow." Initially, I actually turned Wow down. I'm not sure what it was, but it was a "No for me, dawg." LOL! Family is the most important thing to me, so long story short, Wow looked out for my family in a major way later that day. That's how my "no" turned into a "yes."

Fast-forward to a few weeks later...

A few nosey people decided to run their mouths behind my back which, in turn, led to my mother and me figuring out who was going to look at the results of my pregnancy test. Let's note here I had taken one at a friend's house but the second line was **BARELY** visible, so I kinda just ignored it (sorry mom). This test, however, was **clearly** positive. Childddd, I like to damn die! So many emotions ran through me all at once. I think it was just really hard to accept the fact that I—*Jasmine*—at the age of 19 was pregnant. I was actually going to be someone's mom! As if God was really going to trust **ME** with a child?!

It wasn't until my first doctor's appointment that it really sunk in that I was actually pregnant. There's something to be said about hearing your child's heartbeat for the first time and getting a due date...

My due date was July 27, 2009—right after my 20th birthday.

As time went on, I just **KNEW** I was carrying a boy because surely, God wouldn't torture me with a miniature version of myself. My son was going to be everything I imagined. I had it all planned out. His name was going to be Khalil Sincere. We were going to do all types of mommy-and-son dates, wear matching outfits, and the whole nine yards. I was hype! You hear me?

As my pregnancy progressed, so much happened. Wow and I spent time together, with each other's family, and also went to my doctor's appointments.

Time absolutely seemed to fly by. The day finally came when we would find out what we were going to have. Lo and behold, I was wrong as **two** left shoes. We were having a ***girl***! *Talk about being in my feelings!* I have the pictures to prove it. Everyone does. The now-funny photo made the shower invitation. LOL!

After some time, we chose a name for our daughter (no, there was **NOT** one picked before). I told y'all I ***KNEW*** it was a boy! We settled on the name Gabrielle Yunik.

Before I knew it, June came around. It was time for our first of three baby showers! The outpouring of love and support that surrounded us was inexpressible. The number of gifts was ridiculous. I never knew one baby could have so much stuff! It got me *really* excited!

When baby shower number two rolled around, talks of shower number three began and more doctor's appointments were on the horizon. I started to love the idea of being someone's mom. My mother and son dreams slowly switched to mommy and daughter ones. The thought of a 'Mini-Me'—Daddy's Princess—made it all so exciting. The love Gabrielle would have and the support from our families would be immeasurable.

July 17, 2009, was my last appointment before our due date. We were **ten days** away from our lives changing forever—from finally becoming *parents*. We were **ten days** away from locking eyes with Gabrielle. It had become surreal. The last appointment went great! Her heartbeat was strong, her measurements were on point, and mommy was fatter. All was well.

Friday, July 24, 2009—exactly one week after my last appointment—things just didn't feel right. I knew Gabrielle was running out of room to move around, so she wasn't as active. Her movements weren't as frequent. That made me nervous as hell! I called my doctor, and I was assured everything was fine. I kinda relaxed. I started thinking, "Maybe it's all in my mind. Maybe it's nerves." At the time, I was precisely **48 hours** away from giving birth, so maybe I was tripping a little bit.

Later that night, my gut was still feeling funny, so I asked my mom to take me to the emergency room. After all, there was no harm in checking on my baby girl. Once I get settled into a room, my doctor came in and I shared with her my concerns. She proceeded to locate Gabrielle's heartbeat. It felt like an eternity had passed. I watched as my doctor's facial expression slowly started to change. She kept searching and moving the fetal heartbeat monitor around. Still, nothing. She looked at me and said, "Your baby doesn't have a heartbeat."

> *"Your baby doesn't have a heartbeat...*
> *Your baby doesn't have a heartbeat..."*

Although she only said it only once, I swear I heard her repeat it a million times. That was all I heard in the confines of that small room. I saw her lips continue to move but honestly, I heard **nothing** else she said. As far as I was concerned, time literally stood still.

The next few hours were a blur. People came to see me. They cried. They talked to me. They hugged and prayed for me. And then, I was admitted. Physically, I was there; mentally, all I could hear was the doctor repeatedly saying:

"Your baby doesn't have a heartbeat.
Your baby doesn't have a heartbeat."

What did she mean? My baby moved earlier. As a matter-of-fact, she gave me a kick after I drank some orange juice. Gabrielle was fine **just last week**! She had a strong heartbeat. She *always* had a strong heartbeat. At every appointment, the staff always said that about her. How could a strong heartbeat just **stop**? How could it be fine and then not? Just that fast...just like that...nothing. I was **two days** away from my due date. **Just two days!**

That was the start of the worst 24 hours of my life. My labor had to be induced (I was given medication to assist with that). I had to go through the actual process of giving birth. After a long, oddly-calm night of being medicated and falling in and out of sleep, on Saturday, July 25, 2009, at 9:24 a.m., I gave birth to a beautiful baby girl. Holding her lifeless body in my arms was torture. No matter what I said to her...no matter how many times I kissed her...no matter how lovingly I touched her, she would never lock eyes with me. I couldn't hold her close and feel her heartbeat.

My entire pregnancy was spent imagining hearing her heartbeat in person, just like I did through the sonogram. I had imagined her having big, brown, beautiful eyes that you could get lost in. I never had the opportunity to confirm that.

I didn't want to let her go. I didn't want to share her with her dad or our parents. In that moment, I was beyond selfish. I waited to hear her cry, whine, open her eyes, take her first stretch...something. **Anything!** Anything that would show me the night before was a joke or nightmare. None of that ever happened, though. She never moved. She never cried. She never blinked. She just laid there motionless in my arms, her dad's arms, our parents' arms, and in the plastic crib.

Family members came to visit. Some even got us to smile and laugh a little. All the while, I kept my eyes on Gabrielle. I was waiting for an act of God or something else to intercede. I **needed** a miracle to happen and for my baby to do something—*anything*—to wake me from the nightmare that was happening.

The nursing staff came in and stated they had to take my baby away. They gave me a stack of papers to sign and asked what I wanted to do with Gabrielle. What did I **WANT**? I **WANTED** my baby's heart to start beating. I **WANTED** to take my baby home. I **WANTED** to feed her and change those disgusting poop-filled diapers—the kind that goes all the way up her back and through her clothes…the kind that other parents complained about. There was no one in that hospital who could give me what I **WANTED**; no one on this earth, for that matter.

The annoying (but necessary) questions continued, to include: "Do you want to cremate or bury her?" Before I could utter the words that I didn't want her cremated and sprinkled across some random forest, her dad flipped out! He let it be known that burial was the **ONLY** option. Then, they took Gabrielle from my room.

What was I supposed to do? Clearly, my body had given birth, yet there I was without a baby. I was placed into a very nice room, away from the other moms and their babies. I suppose that was done so that I wouldn't hear the other babies' cries. They even let me stay in the hospital a couple of extra nights. Eventually, the time came for me to leave—but not before they sent a thousand people to "give support": counselors, doctors, and even a Lactation Specialist. I was then given a "Memory Box." A freaking **BOX**! How was my child's life supposed to fit inside a **BOX**? What was I supposed to put inside the **BOX**?

When I was released, I was wheeled out of the hospital's doors empty-handed. I had no baby. It was just me and a **BOX**.

Once I returned home, everything was even more difficult to deal with. I had to plan a funeral for Gabrielle Yunik. I've been to funerals throughout the years, but never in a million years did I think I would be responsible for planning one—let alone my child's.

Have you ever had to plan a funeral? The experience was **BEYOND** stressful.

Gabrielle had to have an outfit, someone to carry her...and an infant casket. Infant caskets have to be one of the saddest things **ever** created.

Have you ever had to create an obituary? What does an obituary say for someone who never had a chance to live?

Then, she had to be buried somewhere, right? Hence, the acquisition of my first piece of "property". Who the hell knew that at 20 years old, I would own **property**? And a burial plot, at that? I still have the deed and, to this day, it's still baffling to me that that's the first thing I've ever really purchased and owned. I have cried on that plot of land so many times...so many days. I just sit there with Gabrielle and cry. There are times I look at the deed...and cry.

The funeral itself was a blur. All I remember is staring at her laying in the casket and thinking to myself, "This is really real! She's gone and never coming back. That's my baby—our baby—in a casket. That is where she'll be forever. Time will continue to move forward. Life will go on. And Gabrielle will still be *there*."

Nine years have passed since then. It's still hard as hell to accept the fact that my child's life has been reduced to a Memory Box—and a spot in the ground. Every day is still a challenge. I still see her in my dreams. Even though I know it's just a dream and far from reality, it feels so real. I don't care what others say; time heals ***nothing***. Time simply momentarily distracts you from the pain. Nothing really heals those wounds other than accepting that it's unhealable and part of the process.

You are welcome to follow my continuing journey through my blog. I hope you will.

www.jasminetalisha.com

Jasmine Talisha ~ Dedication

To my children: Gabrielle, Kayden, Jayden, and Peyton. You saved me. Each of you changed my life in ways you could never know. I'll never know what I did right, but I thank God each and every day for the blessings you've all been to me. I love you guys! Thank you for allowing Mommy to be her.

~ *Chavon Winston* ~

Chavon Winston was born in Washington, D.C. where she completed most of her schooling and later received her high school diploma. She is a General Manager and has three daughters with her fiancée.

Chavon's goals include being a Motivational Speaker to those who deal with loss and starting a nonprofit organization for the youth to strengthen and empower them to strive for greatness.

"THE JOURNEY IS WHAT YOU MAKE IT. YOU JUST HAVE TO MAKE THE FIRST STEP!"

Mishia Bee

Double Jeopardy

Talk about an unforgettable memory! I will never forget my mom picking up my brother and I on this dreadful day. The thing that makes **this** day different was that everything about *her* was different. Her attitude, her tone, her every movement was just different. At first, I thought that maybe she was having a bad day, but no: She had bad news.

That day, she explained my dad has been shot. For me, on that day, I didn't know how to process that news. Before that day, I would see my dad on most weekends and holidays. I even lived with him for a period of time. So, it's not like we didn't have a relationship, even though my mom was a single mother. Between the two of them, they made sure we saw not only my dad, but also his side of the family and my other siblings as well.

I was 14 years old and, at that time, I was going through teenage "issues." Losing my dad only made my life that much harder. Yes, I could talk to my mom, but I didn't. I always felt I had more time to build my relationship with my dad. Before that day, I harbored envy toward my brothers because I felt my dad spent more time with them and gave them more leeway. I felt like they had that bond **only** because they were *boys*. I thought if I were a boy, he would treat me different and want to hang out with me more. Don't get me wrong: He never *ignored* me, but I guess he didn't understand that I needed more of him and his time.

Some time after his passing, I got a boyfriend who seemed to give me all the attention I *thought* I was missing. (Now that I'm grown, I realize you can't replace that void. Just acknowledge it and go from there.) Looking back, that's when I realized having "daddy issues" doesn't always come from an **absent** father. He can be right in front of you and still not be as attached as you need him to be. I don't recall my dad ever telling me I was beautiful or even congratulating me on doing anything well. I do, however, remember him helping me with my studies and reading me a few books. I don't remember seeing him at my 6th grade graduation, taking me school shopping, or even giving me "The Talk" about boys.

Looking at him lay in his casket was overwhelming. I couldn't pick him up. I couldn't hug him, hear him say "I love you," or even laugh together one more time. My dad was a very funny man. That's something **anyone** who knew him was guaranteed to say. It's so sad that it was all snatched away just like that.

One day, I was cleaning up and found a picture of my dad when he was a teenager. I began to wonder what his childhood was like. My own was over because I held firm to a feeling of abandonment that I didn't realize I was carrying. I became very hardheaded. There was no explanation for most of the things I started to do. I was sneaking to talk to boys on the phone, knowing my momma would go off on me. But I needed **someone** to say to me all the things I missed and wished I had heard from my dad.

After he passed, I spent less time with his side of the family. It's not that I didn't want to spend time with them, but for me, it was a reminder that he was truly gone (I tried to convince myself that was the reason).

Before that day, I thought I was a happy child. I thought I was centered. School was good and I had decent friends. I was in cheerleading and the band. Everything came to a stop all at once, and I didn't even realize it. I shut down from participating in everything except going to school. I didn't even notice I was hurting that bad. I carried a burden in my younger years about my dad thinking I wasn't good enough. In hindsight, I know my dad had his own way of showing he loved me, which is why his absence affected me the way it did. Had he not helped with homework, read a few books, or made me smile, where would I be? I guess when you step back, you see the picture clearer. I was too young to figure all of that out on my own.

My mom always told me to "Pause." LOL! Now, I get it! She was no joke! **PERIOD!** In my mind, I used to tell myself, "I'm going through something. What does she know? She doesn't understand me." I'd been holding in so much, coupled with the normal pressures of being a teen. Silly me: My mother knew more than I gave her credit for.

She and my dad had my brother and I when they were young. I guess that's why she was always hovering over me. She was **always** a step ahead of me, which is all the more reason why I should have talked to her.

Two years passed. My mom couldn't stand my "boyfriend", but she finally gave in and told me she was okay—which was great because her changing her mind **NEVER, EVER** happened. She said to me, "I'm not going to keep trying to pull you away from him because the more I pull, the more you'll push." Even though she didn't like me having a boyfriend, she accepted the relationship...for me. That was a weight lifted off of me because I no longer had to hide anything from my mom—and I didn't. I hated keeping secrets from her but felt I had to because with my mom, no means no—**PERIOD**!

Mom was very fun, very present, and also very strict and aware. She didn't allow me to go out much, especially without an adult or my brother, so we would have parties at my house to distract me from envying the freedoms my friends had. We hosted sleepovers, girls' night, game night, and other fun activities.

At around age 9 or 10, I learned how to cook, do laundry, and take care of myself. It seemed like every weekend, my brother and I were cleaning up the house. I used to think my mom had Obsessive Compulsive Disorder, but I now know she was grooming and preparing us for life. Although I have siblings from a different mother, ours made sure they came over and that we had a relationship with them. Man, I hated when she used to take my sister's side when we would fight or when she made me give away my stuff. I didn't realize she was showing me how to be fair and not show favoritism just because I was **her** daughter. It seemed like I was just starting to understand how important it was to have her as my mom. Not only did she help shape my life; she purposely shaped me to be the **best** me—not just a young woman, but one with substance, morals, and self-respect.

I didn't truly get it, though. I didn't understand. I thought it was all about her power to say "no." Well, she was saying "no" for a reason. Those **"NOs"** had purpose and meaning.

Then, one day, mom said she was ill and had to be admitted into the hospital. She came home a few days later. Although I visited with her in the hospital, her being back home was the best!

My 16th birthday was coming, and mom spared no expense. I had a live go-go band, she rented the local rec center, and all my friends, most of the neighborhood, and my family were there. It was the best party ever! I will never forget it.

A couple of days later, mom was readmitted to the hospital. This time, she stayed for a few weeks. This time, she came home on hospice care. She wasn't going to be with us much longer, and there was nothing I could do about it. I did my best to make her comfortable. I rubbed down her body every day and night before bed. Anything she asked for, I gave. It was exhausting and sad to see her in that condition. She started to lose weight fast, mostly because she didn't want to eat. Her body was sore, mostly because she wasn't moving around much anymore. I didn't know what to do with myself when I wasn't home. So, I started back hanging out. I was confused because her illness seemed to come out of nowhere. I could never leave her alone too long because she needed **me** the most. In my mind, I cried out, "It's not fair! I'm only a child! What am I supposed to do?"

One day, I was so overwhelmed with it all and went out to take a long walk alone. No one I knew could relate to my plight. I really didn't know how to talk about it, even though I needed *someone* to understand!

A couple of weeks went by. Mom was having a "good day" and so was I. I hung out with my friends and stayed out a little later than I should have. I also did a few things I shouldn't have and knew I had to talk to my mom about it. No matter her condition, I promised her I wouldn't lie to her. On this day, I had to tell her I lost my virginity. I didn't know how to verbalize it, so I wrote her a note instead. I stayed in my room for most of that day until she called me down. I just **KNEW** I was "dead on arrival" because no matter the condition of her health, I still respected her—and she still let me know what she expected from me. So, we had a talk.

During the conversation, she explained to me not just about *sex*, but also all that comes with it. She said, "You can't **look** at people and know what's wrong with them—and don't expect them to just come out and tell you. Always protect and respect yourself. And, because I'm sure you'll do it again, protect yourself not just for you, but also for the other person. Sex isn't just 'fun'; it's also dangerous. So, always be safe." We had a long talk that night, and she enlightened me on why she was so hard on me and why she kept me away from so many things I thought were simply (in my mind) "fun."

About a month after that, she stopped talking altogether—not because she didn't want to talk, but because her health had gotten that bad. I then lost my voice of reason. Yes, I had friends, but **mom** was my diary. Yes, I could still talk **TO** her, but she couldn't respond. *It wasn't fair!*

The day was October 3, 2014. I was sitting upstairs in my room with my cousin when I heard her mom scream. I just dropped my head and closed my eyes. I didn't say a word for what seemed like forever. Eventually, I got up and went downstairs. That was it. Mom was gone. My best friend—the one who was supposed to see me graduate high school, have children, and get married—was gone. I lost it all. Now, what?

It seemed everyone knew what was best for me. They transferred my school and tried to change **everything** about me after my mom passed away. All of their efforts did nothing but make me feel even **more** alone, out of place, sheltered, and, most of all, angry! My emotions went all over the place. While everyone had "my best interests at heart," they all forgot the most important thing: how I was feeling and what I may have been going through. No one took the time out to ask, "Hey! How is your day?" They just moved me around and assumed I would adapt. That's how I was left to feel because once she was in the ground, my world became foreign to me.

I was all alone with nothing or no one to turn to. Sometimes, my own feet would fail me as I thought about all of what happened to me. My world flipped inside out and I had no idea what to do next.

As I tried to cope with my loss in my own way, I likely pushed some people away from me—not because I felt I didn't need them, but more because they weren't there when I needed the support. My actions spoke louder than ever, which was misinterpreted as me being a problem-child who was lashing out. Strange thing: No one ever seemed to make the *proper* connection.

So, as my young life continued, I carried a hatred that I never truly released. I never actually released my mom from my heart because I never fully accepted the fact that she was never coming back—**EVER!** I just couldn't. Surely, my days got better, but sometimes I still stumbled with every accomplishment or milestone. Mom was never far from my thoughts. Even something as simple as a song on the radio brought up the fact that I lost not one, but both parents. I was just a child. That wasn't the way it was supposed to be, right?

As I maneuver life's obstacles, I keep my parents in mind. I try to remember the good times. Although I shed a few tears from time to time, I acknowledge that I can't change the past. What I **CAN** do is take all that I've learned from them and carry **THOSE** things with me. It took some time, but day by day, I find strength.

Now that I have children of my own, my parents come to mind more than ever. Instead of that loneliness I had, I feel so grateful. Although my parents left too soon, I have so many things to give my children to provide them guidance in my absence. So, with this hard life lesson, I have truly learned a great deal at such a young age. While I raise my daughters, I may give them those same "NOs" with the added benefit of sharing the reason **why** behind them. I will always say "I love you" with the feelings to match. I will be their diaries without judgment.

I gained something from both of my parents and didn't realize it until, in my opinion, it was too late. I realized it when I was finally ready for whatever life has for me next. When I leave this earth, I pray my daughters have gained great things from me to pass on to their children. There isn't a book in the world that can teach you how to be a good parent, but as long as you give it your all and your best, you've done plenty.

So, I thank my mom and dad because looking back, I believe they gave me **all** they had...*and then some.*

I'm not sure if I will ever stop shedding tears with an occasional smile attached. I do know that with time comes ease and understanding. I've gained peace and acceptance. My core is no longer as hard as a rock. As life goes on, my parents will be forever in my heart. Death doesn't always mean "The End."

Thanks, Mom & Dad! ♥

Chavon Winston ~ Dedication

I would like to dedicate this to the Most High GOD first for allowing me the strength to tell my story. To my family and my children, K.M.K.: With your love, you've given me courage to even begin writing the first line.

Kahil: Thanks, Babe, for being my rock and my peace. All the love and support you give really matter. Thank you!

~ JessMarie ~

JessMarie is a native of Tarboro, North Carolina. She is an Air Force Veteran and currently works as a Therapeutic Behavior Aide within the D.C. charter schools. Jessica has a passion for children and hopes to one day inspire them through her motivational speaking.

JessMarie is the mother of an 18-year-old daughter, Esence, and 16-year-old son, Jordan. She recently became engaged to her fiancée, Paul. She loves singing, traveling, and making others laugh.

Mishia Bee

Not All Scars Are Visible

"Get up! Get up! It's time for y'all to get ready for school, so get yourselves together." As a high school senior, those words should have resonated so loudly that I would have jumped for joy! Unfortunately, that wasn't the case for me. I did not want to be bothered with the "Hey, Skinny Minny!" or "There goes 'Hair and Legs'!" taunts. I would be so hurt listening to what others thought of me. The stuff they said as a "joke" only served to further lower the 'S' in my self-esteem. Of course, high school is not when this all began. I dealt with it during middle school as well.

Let's take a trip down Memory Lane...

August 1988 ushered in my 5th grade year at Martin Middle School, which is located in my hometown of Tarboro, North Carolina. See, I wasn't very popular. I'm not sure why not, especially since I have always considered myself a people-person. I never meet a stranger to this day. If someone approaches me with conversation, they would definitely have my undivided attention. I came to realize it's not because I **wouldn't** talk; I was just different.

As you could probably figure out by now, I have always been petite and lanky. Never would someone equate me with the adjective "thick." It took an act of

Congress for me to grow boobs, but then I would cover them up because I could not fathom the humiliation. I would find myself asking my parents why I wasn't built like my friends. I desperately wanted to be shapely. Their response to my inquiry would always be, "You are absolutely fine the way you are." The thing my parents didn't understand at the time was that I couldn't care less about what **they** thought. They had to love me as I am. I needed *society* to accept me as I am.

My low self-esteem led me to do things just for attention. Now, don't judge me. I will admit those things weren't always peaches and cream. Things like what, you ask? Well, let me say this: If I knew then what I know now—that allowing a guy to come over on teacher workday or skipping school in my senior year or trying to be someone I wasn't—was not going to equate to self-worth, it never would have happened. I would probably still be pure and innocent and would not have released my womanhood to a young man I never saw again, all because I wanted to fit in. I toy with this issue now, but through growth and a lot of tears, coping is much easier.

See, if you don't accept JessMarie as she is, you can't hold a position in her life. I know my worth. I am someone, and opinions from counterparts, coworkers, or total strangers will never define me as a person.

I'm my parents' oldest child. I have a brother who is three years younger than me. He was the 'cool kid.' To this day, my brother is my best friend and diary. We have so many secrets, but I'm sure he had **no** idea his sister was battling with an issue internally. His friends (all male, of course) would be pie in my hands whenever they came over to visit. I made sure I was in the mix because I wanted that attention. I would do stuff just for them to notice me walking by. And, of course, if they *didn't* notice, I would be **crushed**.

You see, I thought being noticed was all it took to boost my self-esteem. All it ended up doing was diminish my self-love. I had to learn that it's not the outside that determines my self-worth; it's the inner beauty that shines outwardly that people notice.

Still, we all know that as a teenager/young adult, we want to be known for a pretty face, big behind, long hair, etc. I didn't engage with teen or pre-teen girls because I did not fit in. I just knew I would always be the center of attention—but not in the way that I wanted. I wanted to be "her." Who is "her"? **She** is Miss

Congeniality. **She** is Miss Superlative. **She** is Miss Popularity. Why wasn't I "her"?

During adolescence, we have so many things that we are dealing with internally. Even with an avenue to address them, the situations do not truly subside; they only fester into something bigger that some, like myself, carry into young adulthood and beyond.

As you can see, this topic is one I hold dear because of my experiences. I hope to one day apply every lesson I've learned during my growth to help every man, woman, and child encompass their self-worth.

Self-esteem is defined as confidence in one's own worth or abilities. Self-esteem is an inner trait that adjectives such as confidence, pride, and security all intertwine to show how one feels about their whole person. For several individuals (to include myself), this is an ongoing battle. I often find myself reflecting on how I found coping mechanisms to confirm that I am okay. It's okay that I'm shaped in a thin, petite frame, while my sister-girl is curvaceous. I now know that diversity is shaped by choices. If every single woman in the world was built the same, where would the differences or, for our men, *choices* be? If every woman had long hair, how could we learn a new style? As time passed, maturation helped me learn that I am my own fan, my own critic, and that my own opinion is what matters. It's okay to be different. It's okay to have your own identity.

"Hey, Jess! You are looking like a million bucks!"

I smile at the compliments I receive and often follow up my thoughts with, "Thank You, God!" I have come a long way, and I didn't get to where I am alone. It took some praying, some tear-shedding, some talking to my parents, and some talking to my good girlfriends/sisters to understand just how awesome I am. I take pride in my past because I can see my growth. I have children who need their self-worth instilled in them. I did not want them to fathom half the thoughts I endured when I was younger. I find myself constantly speaking words of encouragement into them and making sure they are certain that they are somebody. They are handsome. They are cute. They are smart. They are talented. And guess what? It's okay that society may not feel the same. Let society have their opinion!

This project was enlightening. It brought forth some reminiscing and I fought back many tears, but I wouldn't change a thing about the process. Each one of us are dealing with things in life that are not abnormal, but we want our stories to reach and teach. Do I still sometimes deal with issues of confidence? Indeed, I do! I may get dressed and change clothes a million times, all while saying, "This doesn't look right." I then check myself and flip it: "Jess, it does look right! It's gorgeous on you!"

Uplift and embrace yourself from the inside out. People whom you encounter always see the confidence you wear. Even when you suppose they are not watching you, they are. You are worth watching!

In my environment, I'm aware that self-esteem is not a stranger. Our cousins, spouses, parents, and children fight this battle as well. My experience with this was not easy and sometimes, I still find myself faced with challenges. That's life! I often monitor my response because there may be a younger version of me watching. I vow to teach them by my actions, body language, and the words I use in my responses. I vow to one day tell my story to women all around and leave them knowing it's okay and that **everyone** is entitled. We are not going to be everyone's "cup of tea." I will teach that your worth is not determined by what others think; rather, it's determined by what *you* think. The pride that I display in my actions when I recall my past causes me to smile.

Self-esteem relates to what I thought of myself, and I made those around me agree with what I thought of myself. Now that I'm older and have matured a bit, I say to myself, "You had it all wrong." It's called **self-esteem**, not ***our-esteem***. Although people will say what they feel, we can never let that determine what we think of our whole person.

I am someone. I am Miss Congeniality. I am Miss Superlative. I am Miss Popularity. I am "HER"!

I read a saying once that said, "Work on being in love with the person in the mirror who has been through much but is still standing" (author unknown). In the process of adapting and overcoming, I learned to do exactly what the quote advised. I learned to love me **entirely**. I learned to embrace everything about me from every aspect of life and noticed that I began to carry around a level of confidence that left **no** room for negativity when it came to the thoughts of others.

People only have as much power over me as I give them. Sticks and stones may break my bones, but words will never **MAKE** me (I switched the word to apply to my personal situation). I have grown!

I would like to leave you, the reader, with this thought: Self-esteem is an inner feeling. It is thoughts that you—as an individual—think of you. Regardless of how a statement or comment someone makes causes you to feel, you push! Keep repeating, "I am someone! I am worth it all!" Your newfound self-esteem you carry around will not be shaken or moved. It's yours. It belongs to you!

JessMarie ~ Dedication

I dedicate this book to my family and to everyone in the world who thinks they are not good enough! You are, and you will always be. Dance to the beat of your own drum and sing to the tune of your own music!

~ Jasmine Hubbard ~

Jasmine Hubbard is a mother of two and was born in Northwest Washington, D.C. She has a passion for inspiring our youth. Jasmine's vision is to both help and guide youths to excellence.

Jasmine believes that no matter the background or home setting, success can be achieved. She aspires to start a mentoring/motivational nonprofit organization for our youth.

Seeking My New Normal

"**How** are you going to be real with anyone if you can't be real with yourself? Know who **YOU** are!"

My story is somewhat unique. I didn't come from a troubled background. I had all the family and friends I needed, but felt like I had no support. As a child, I always felt a little *different*. I didn't know if it was me or how my family interacted with me that made me feel that way. I can remember being really "busy"—what some would call "hyper." I also remember saying the first thing that came to mind…and sometimes getting in trouble for doing so. With that combination of traits, I was labeled the "problem child."

I recall things being said about me such as, "It's always you." Now, I don't want to discredit those who love me the most. I know they love me dearly. Still, my parents weren't as lenient as others. I often felt like my friends had more freedoms than I did. (As it turned out, I am truly blessed by that because I turned out to be a decent, young woman.) Around my middle school years, I started to feel a disconnect. I was always getting into some type of trouble no matter how big or small, even at family gatherings.

I have a close cousin whom I love with all my heart. She's a lot like a sister to me. I always felt I was compared to her. She made better grades, behaved better, and didn't talk back. Whatever the case may be, in my eyes, she was the "Golden Child." I was "Lil Miss Can't-Get-Right." LOL! I can reflect and make jokes *now* because my mind is no longer in that space. Nonetheless, because of that mindset, I was always on the defense in my childhood—which caused me to be argumentative with those who loved me and wanted what was best for me.

At a young age, I was diagnosed with Attention Deficit Hyperactivity Disorder. I can't pinpoint **exactly** when, but I believe it was around the age of five or six. I can recall being told to go take my chill-pills and being asked, "You didn't take your medicine?" I now know it might have been said in a joking manner but as a child, I began to feel like *something* was wrong with me. At the time, I don't know if what I was feeling was visible to everyone around me, but my parents would give me pep talks before family functions just to try to prepare me and have my behavior checked at the door. Somehow, I **always** found a way to get into trouble. It was as if it was expected of me to do something that prompted the "Here we go!" response.

As children, we're taught the adult is always right. I remember getting into trouble because I was (in my eyes) defending myself from two altercations with family members. I wasn't disrespectful in the way like you might be thinking. I didn't tell adults I wasn't going to do something that was required of me. I wasn't going around cussing them out, either. Still, as a child, whatever the viewpoint adults had of me caused me to miss out on activities such as going to concerts or hanging out with certain people.

In all honesty, I can say I don't know if my mother felt or saw how I was feeling, but she did make sure I wanted for nothing. She gave me anything I asked for.

Around the 5th or 6th grade, my mother started dating a new guy. Eventually, she got pregnant by him. I was happy...at first. When the baby came, I felt even **more** out of place. It was as if *they* had a family, and I was "just there"...an outsider.

That lonely feeling continued for years, to the point that I never wanted to attend family events. I didn't feel like being the one always doing something wrong. As I grew older, my defensive nature became my normal attitude. I was always uptight and feeling like I had to prove I was no one's f**k-up!

At the age of 18, I got pregnant and had a baby. At the age of 24, I gave birth to my second child. Even then, I believe I was viewed in a dull light. With those feelings bearing down on me, I knew how I wanted to raise **my** family. Just like that, my main focus changed. I felt that in order to survive, that change was my key to a successful life. I had a need to find a spouse and move on. With that mindset, I found myself jumping head over heels into relationships (or should I say "feelings"). LOL! I would put all my eggs in one basket and get my *feelings* hurt because I thought everyone had the same agenda as me…when they didn't.

When I was 25 years old, I met my first real (well, what I **thought** was real) love. You couldn't tell me he wasn't my Prince Charming! He was just coming home from lockup *(that should have been a red flag)*. I believed we could help each other. I was **so** in love with him that either I couldn't see the red flags or simply didn't care. After all, I had *finally* found my other half to walk with me through life. He showered me with so much affection. Soon after, we ended up getting a place together. Not long after that, I learned our little, happy family wasn't so happy after all.

2016 was one tough and trying year. I was determined to make our little family work. I allowed my children to witness me accepting things and behaviors that **no** woman with a man by her side should have to endure. In response, I had lost so much weight due to the stress of trying to take care of my family with little to no help from him.

As things between he and I started to fall apart, my child's father started contacting me again (while he was locked up). *(That should have been **another** red flag.)* The only time he seemed to know my number was when he was behind bars. I never engaged in pillow talk about my current relationship with him because 1: I was embarrassed, and 2: I didn't want him to know what I was dealing with. My then-boyfriend and I had a toxic relationship. We ended up losing our apartment, which resulted in me having to move back uptown with my father. Soon after, things came to an end with my then-boyfriend.

The more I talked to my child's father, the more we would talk about 'us.' Now, I don't know if I was vulnerable at the time and on the rebound or if I truly believed with everything in me that we were meant to be. He and I talked daily. Once again, I found myself placing all my eggs in one basket without considering the odds. I dove right in, thinking this was **it** for me. **This** was my ticket to surviving and having a normal family life. Mind you: He was still incarcerated while we were 'rebuilding.' However, there I was with **all** the confidence in the world that this man would come home and make all my situations better somehow.

2017 ushered in yet **another** difficult year. Around this time, I was going through a lot. Once I moved back in with my father, I learned about the troubles he and my aunt were dealing with. It was determined that my aunt would reside in a nursing home. Insurance didn't cover all the costs, so the facility wanted collateral...the house. The additional debt caused us to get an eviction notice.

At the same time, I was putting forth efforts to get "my man" home to complete my golden family. You know...the All-American Dream! *Yeah, right!* LOL! Mom, dad, daughter, and son—with plans for **additional** add-ons. LOL! I can laugh now at how wide open my nose was. Well, I **FINALLY** got him home! I was so excited! Despite what anyone said, I just *knew* my moment had arrived.

Wait. How is it possible that he's home, yet once again, I still feel alone? I had my expectations set far too high. I ended up disappointed and tried making excuses for him such as, "Well, when you met him, he was in the streets. That's just who he is."

Listen up: No matter what a person is doing, people make time for who and what they want to make time for. Never **EVER** make excuses for them.

As for "my man", if he wanted better, he would have done something different. We clashed heads about everything, especially when it came down to him doing his part. I often found myself with the weight of the world on my shoulders due to my frustration with his lack of effort and communication. That led to arguments, which started to push him away from me. As long as I was okay with how he moved, all was well. As soon as I asked for understanding and respect, I was shut down which caused me to lash out. No, I don't claim to have always been right; however, I **do** claim to be human. As for him, he wasn't the argumentative type and never held himself accountable, so he chose to leave me. That crushed my world. I was hurt and embarrassed. I held out so much hope about 'us.' I was moreso hurt because no matter what, I needed him and his support more than ever (or so I thought). He couldn't or didn't want to see the bigger picture.

NOTE: Communication is the key to success for *any* type of relationship.

At that point, I didn't want to do anything more. I was sick with myself. I had all the time in the world to sit and think. My thoughts turned towards thinking maybe it wasn't him (or them); maybe it was **me**. I was shown signs but because of my want for stability and comfort, I ignored them. I worked diligently to be his "Ride-or-Die, Down-Ass B***h" (excuse my language).

I came to realize I had to get my prescription for life and success right for my children and me. I sought to think differently. I craved a different mindset. Obviously, the one I was operating with wasn't working. If I wanted different results, I had to change some things.

I asked myself, "What is it that I, Jasmine Hubbard, want out of life? What do I want to do with myself? What's my purpose and passion?"

I have always loved children. I also knew I loved to help people. I just didn't know how I was going to turn my love into a career. I realized I didn't have to have a spouse or "complete family" to be successful in life. All I needed was a clear mind, determination, and a hunger to be successful! I had to get out of that dark place.

I knew I wanted to help children who felt like me or who looked at life a different way, no matter their background. I wanted to help children strive for better, no matter what was thrown their way. I can remember hearing adults ask, "Where's their mother?" when they noticed children misbehaving. The proactive thing to do would have been to talk to the children to learn **why** they were acting out. Some children might be motherless or have a mother who is always working just to provide for her children.

As a matter-of-fact, now that I think about it, I don't recall **EVER** being asked, "What's going on with you? Why are you acting like that?" I don't remember **EVER** being asked, "How do you feel about 'x,y,z'?"

Considering that I felt like I could relate to "problem children" on a personal level and all that was going on in their little world, I came up with an idea to open a mentoring and motivational program for our youth. Some children just need a loving push—not a poking or pointing out what they did wrong. Children have feelings and, if not sorted out or expressed in the right way, they become unbalanced *adults* in society. No matter the situation, a child can always use a listening ear or helpful advice instead of immediate judgment. I desire to show them that life is really what you make it and that their success isn't determined by the support they want or think they have (or even *don't* have). It's all up to them. Success is determined by how bad they want it.

See, I believe things happen for a reason. Before those few difficult years, I really couldn't tell you what I wanted in life or what my purpose in life was. I just went through life living day by day, not really planning for my future. Once I had my first child, I tightened up a *little*, but I still didn't have a clue about real "life-life." LOL! These past years have taught me that you win some; you lose some. It's up to you. No matter what, just have **FAITH!**

My tribulations have helped me recognize my purpose. If I can give at least **one** child the comfort of belonging, guide them to their purpose, and let them know **at least one** person can relate to them and care, I've done my part. I also desire to reassure them that they, too, have a **VOICE!**

Jasmine Hubbard ~ Dedication

I dedicate this to my children. I try my best to lead and be a good example of how to never give up. No matter how hard the wind blows, stay steady. XOXO

I would also like to dedicate this chapter to a friend I lost recently: Jasmine Simmons. She was the true definition of a *friend*. She was a helping hand when needed and always found a way to stay positive for herself and others.

"Beauty is power;

a smile is its sword."

~ John Ray ~

Retrieved from:
https://www.brainyquote.com/lists/topics/top_10_smile_quotes

Mishia Bee

www.ingramcontent.com/pod-product-compliance
Lightning Source LLC
Chambersburg PA
CBHW050203130526
44591CB00034B/2064